MORE PIANO SOLOS in a
LYRICAL STYLE

BY CAROLYN MILLER

ISBN 978-1-5400-0220-4

WILLIS MUSIC

EXCLUSIVELY DISTRIBUTED BY

HAL•LEONARD®

7777 W. BLUEMOUND RD. P.O. BOX 13819 MILWAUKEE, WI 53213

Visit Hal Leonard Online at
www.halleonard.com

FROM THE COMPOSER

I explored different emotions while composing these eight pieces, and it is my hope that some will touch the heart while others capture the imagination.

Melodies must be shaped and balanced with the accompaniment. This especially applies to "Deep Thoughts," which is one of my favorites to perform.

It is my hope that students will play these pieces artistically and expressively.

Enjoy!

Carolyn Miller holds music degrees from the College Conservatory of Music at the University of Cincinnati and Xavier University. She has taught piano to students of all ages for many years, both privately and in the classroom. She regularly presents workshops throughout the United States and adjudicates at music festivals and competitions. Carolyn's music teaches essential technical skills, yet is fun to play, which appeals to both children and adults. Many of her compositions appear on contests lists, including the NFMC Festivals Bulletin. Well-known television personality Regis Philbin performed her "Rolling River" and "Fireflies" in 1992 and 1993 on national television.

In her spare time Carolyn directs a large church choir and plays piano for special services. She enjoys spending time with her family, especially her seven grandchildren, each of whom have their own special published piano piece.

CONTENTS

Deep Thoughts

for Kathleen Jendrusik

Carolyn Miller

Dizzy Fingers

Carolyn Miller

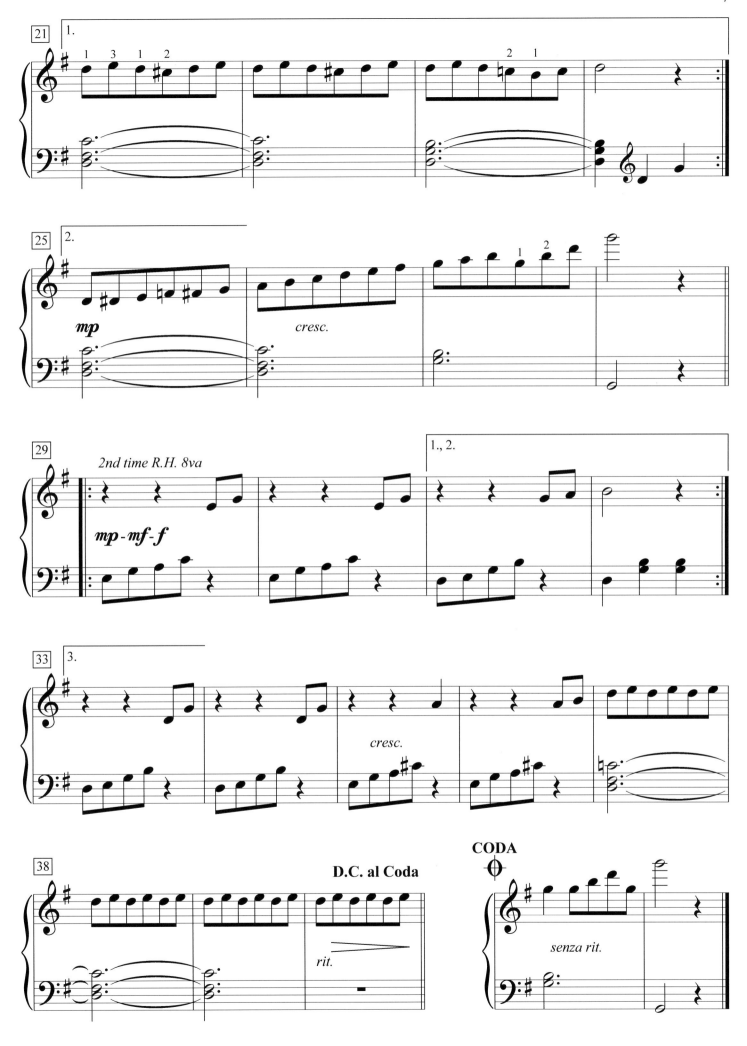

Knights of the Kingdom

Carolyn Miller

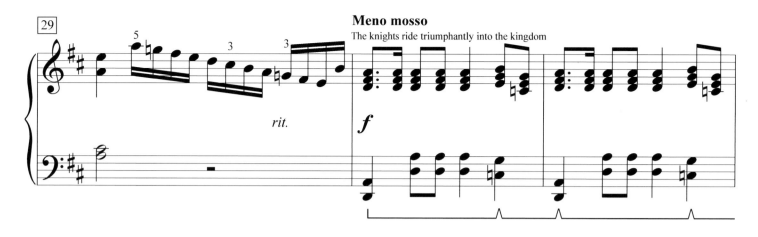

Meno mosso
The knights ride triumphantly into the kingdom

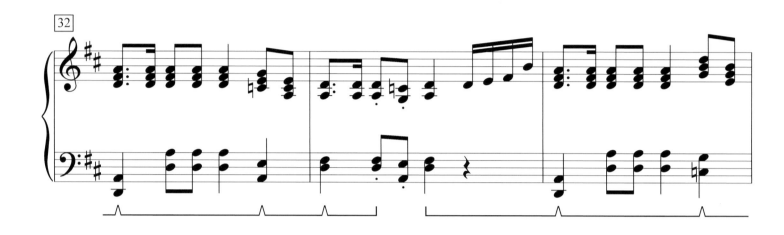

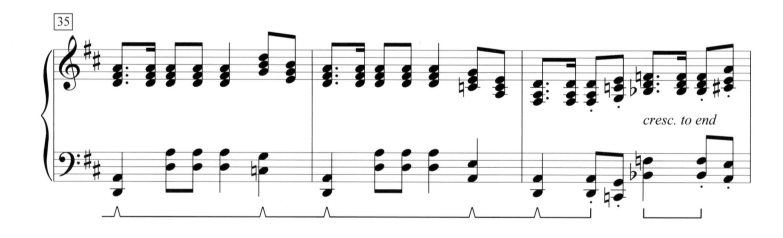

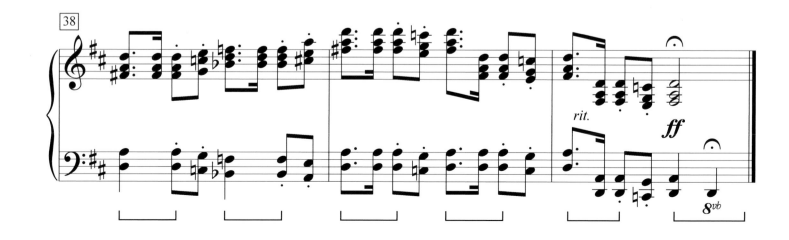

Little Tango

Carolyn Miller

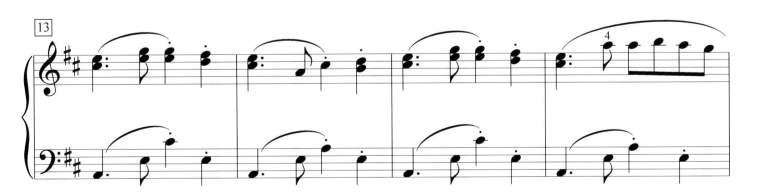

Matter of Fact

Carolyn Miller

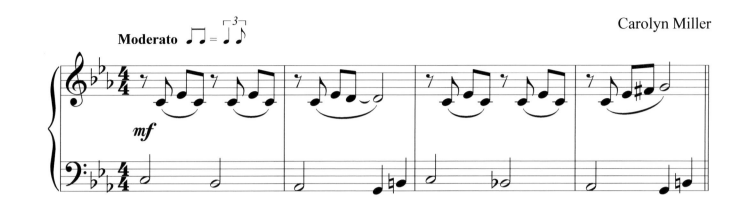

Meditation in G

Carolyn Miller

Simplicity

Carolyn Miller

Storybook Waltz

Carolyn Miller